MAKING THINGS
from
ODDS and ENDS

Written and illustrated by
HOWARD MELL & ERIC FISHER

SCHOFIELD & SIMS LTD · HUDDERSFIELD

First Printed 1969
Reprinted 1970
Reprinted 1973
Reprinted 1974

Printed in Great Britain by
W. S. Cowell Ltd at the Butter Market, Ipswich

Contents

A Word of Advice

You will find that you can enjoy making the things in this book much more if you remember some simple rules:

Before you begin: always cover your desk with newspaper. Put out the things you need.

When you are working: do not let things get too messy.

When you have finished: clean the things you have used and put them away. Put scraps in the wastepaper basket.

Keep things tidy – including yourself!

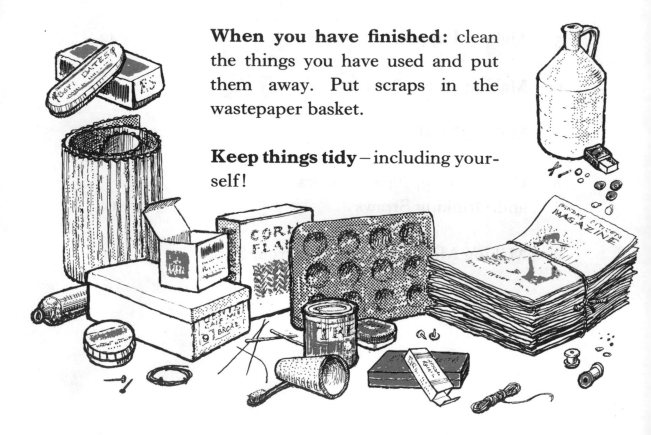

Every day, a lot of things are thrown away.

Sometimes they are put in dustbins, sometimes they are burned.

Sometimes they are left in a drawer or a cupboard.

They have usually been used or are bits and pieces left over when something has been made.

So they could be pieces of wood, cardboard boxes, newspapers, magazines and so on.

Sometimes there are a few nails or buttons, odd pieces of wire or wool left over when a job is finished.

I am sure you can think of a lot of things like this.

They are called "odds and ends".

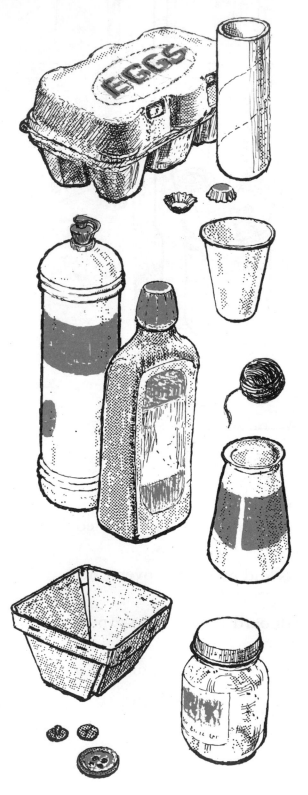

This is a book about making all sorts of things from odds and ends. They can usually be found at home or begged from shops and stores. They might come from mills or factories, workshops or farms. Many of them are exciting to find because they are different from the usual things we work with.

See what you can find. Perhaps you can keep them in a box until you want to use them. Here and there you may have to use things which have been bought, like glue, but mainly you will use odds and ends.

Some of the easiest things to find are newspapers and magazines. They can be used in many different ways. Try some of them!

1. *Making and Using Papier Mâché*

Have you seen those words before — "papier mâché"? They arc French. You can probably guess what "papier" means. Yes! It means "paper". And what about "mâché"? Say it like mash-ay. Does it sound a little like "mashed" in *mashed* potato? Mâché really means "chewed"; so then we get "chewed paper".

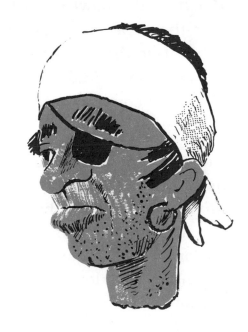

But I am not going to ask you to *chew* paper! You can make papier mâché by tearing the paper. You mash it or *mâché* it without putting it in your mouth.

When you have made it, you will have something you can shape easily with your hands. It dries hard. You can paint it when it is dry.

There are many ways of making it.
Here is an easy one.

You will need :
    Some old newspapers.
    A bowl or bucket.
    Cold water paste.

Tear up the newspaper into *very small* pieces. Put them in the bowl or bucket as you tear them. If you work with other children you will get on faster. Mix the paste – you will soon find out how thin it needs to be.

Put it in the bowl with the paper. Stir the paper and paste together. When I do this, I use my hands, or a big spoon. Make sure all the pieces get covered with paste.

You can help to make the mâché more quickly by squeezing the mixture. Squeeze a handful hard. Let it go and take another handful. Go on squeezing and stirring until you have a nice lot of soggy paper in the bowl.

Put some sheets of newspaper near the bowl. If you have an old piece of card or hardboard, you can use that.

Take a handful of the mixture. Hold it over the bowl. Squeeze it hard, *as hard as you can.* Use both hands. Squeeze several times. Try to get as much paste as you can out of it. SQUEEZE! Are you keeping your hands over the bowl?

When you have squeezed the paper, put it on the newspaper or board. Go on taking more mixture and squeezing it. Put it with the other lumps.

When you have enough papier mâché to make your model, ask your teacher if it is dry enough to use right away. It may need to be a little drier than you have made it. One way to help you make it dry quickly is to mix in a little plaster as you stir the mâché.

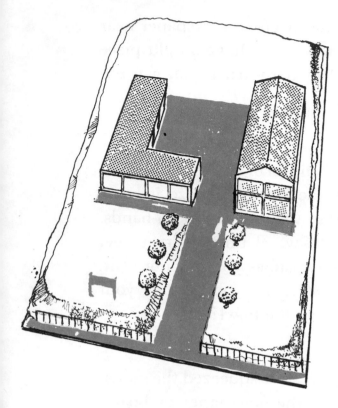

Using papier mâché

Work on a piece of card or hardboard. Or you can use sheets of newspaper. Take the mâché as you need it, and push it or press it into the shapes you want. You can join lumps of it just by pushing them hard together.

When you have made what you want, leave it until it is dry. Then you can colour it if you wish. If you want, you can add things to your model before it dries. The faces on page 7 have raffia and pieces of drinking straw added. Can you see them?

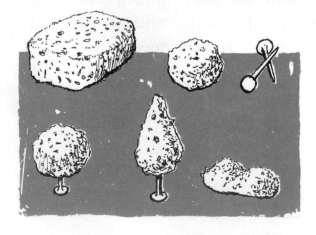

The other pictures on these pages show things made with papier mâché. The model of the school was made by a whole class. Some children measured the sizes. The building was made from card and balsa wood. The trees were an old sponge and some nails.

What are *you* going to make?

Papier mâché can be used to make heads for puppets or dolls.

Roll a piece of thin cardboard into a cylinder and glue it. Do you know what a cylinder is? You can find out or, perhaps, guess by looking at the drawing here. Make the cylinder so that it slides easily over your finger.

Now build up an egg shape on the end of the cylinder using the papier mâché. Put on a nose and a chin and anything else you would like to add. Are you going to make ears? When you have finished, put the head on one side to dry.

When it is finished, you can paint it. You can put on wool or string or straw to make hair.

If you want, you could add a body made of papier mâché or fasten the head into a body to make a puppet. You can read about this on page 42.

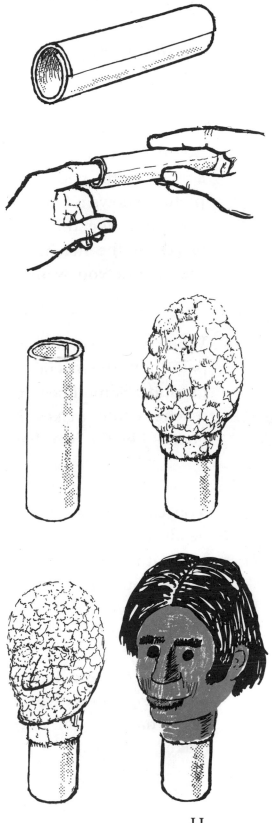

11

Modelling papier mâché on card

You can work on cardboard, hard-board or thick paper to make flat shapes with papier mâché. The picture shows a figure and a motor car made like this. Just push the pieces of the mâché together into the shapes you want.

When your work is dry, you can paint both the mâché and the back-ground. Sometimes, painting the mâché white makes it look very good – like the man here.

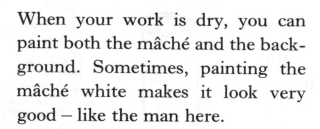

You can have a lot of fun making heads like these in the drawings. Look at the funny faces! They have things pushed into the mâché. Others are glued on when it is dry.

Faces like these look good when they are painted. See what you can do. What else can you think of to make?

2. Working on a Mould

I wonder if you know what a "mould" is? Look up "mould" in your dictionary and talk about it with your teacher.

Have you made sand pies? If you are a girl, perhaps you have made *real* pies or tarts. In the picture opposite, you can see some sand pies made by using a bucket. Underneath are some tarts baked in tart tins. The bucket made the *shape* of the pies. The tart tin made the *shape* of the tarts. The bucket and the tin were used to *shape* or *mould* these things. So we use a *mould* to make a shape.

Can you think of other things which are made in a mould? I can think of puddings, bricks, jellies and toy soldiers. What can you add to these?

Can you find a book about moulding?

You can make shapes on moulds very easily with newspaper. You can use several things for moulds: bowls, wastepaper bins, bottles and so on. The picture shows a washing-up bowl. Yes! It *is* upside down. Notice that it is standing on some newspaper.

If you haven't a washing-up bowl, perhaps you have another sort of bowl or basin. You may want to try a tin can. What have you got?

This is how to continue:

You will need:
 Some newspaper or magazines.
 Toilet paper.
 Paste and paste brush (a big one if you have it).
 Some water.

Have you put plenty of newspaper on your table? Take a piece of toilet paper. Wet it. Put it on the bowl.

Pat it with your fingers to make the paper flat. Water makes this easy. Why is this? What has the water done to the paper?

Put on another piece of toilet paper so that the edge overlaps the first piece. The picture shows you how.

Go on adding more pieces until the bowl is covered. Don't forget to overlap them.

Now you have finished with the water. Are you going to take it away so that you do not make a mess?

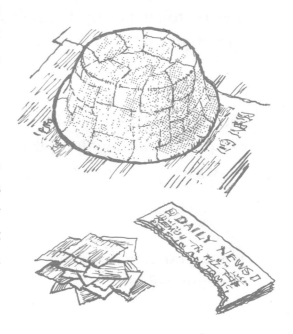

Tear some of the newspaper into pieces. About ten centimetres square. But the size is not very important – see that they are not too big or too small. You will soon see why.

Paste the pieces on top of the toilet paper on the bowl. Make them overlap. Paste them down well. Can you see why the pieces must not be too big?

Cover all the bowl. Then paste on a layer of toilet paper. Have you done that? Now paste on another layer of newspaper. You have put on two layers of each sort of paper. Now paste on another layer of toilet paper and another of newspaper. How many layers is that?

To finish the layers, put on another one of toilet paper. Press it down well if you want to make it smooth.

Put the bowl away until the paper is dry. I wonder how long it will take to dry?

Have you tidied up any mess you have made?

What to do when the paper is dry

Is the paper dry? If it really *is* dry, you should be able to pull off the paper, in one big shape, from the bowl. Get some help if you need it.

Have you got the shape off the bowl? Can you say why you used wet paper to start with? What would happen if you *pasted* the first layer on to the bowl?

Now that you have your paper shape, what are you going to make with it? Perhaps you had already made up your mind? Talk about your ideas with your teacher.

The pictures show a castle and a hat made with moulds. Can you guess what was used as a mould in each case?

17

Once you have tried working on moulds, you will soon do better and get more ideas. Try painting and adding things to your shapes. Look at the hat, it has something fastened to it. Try putting different shapes together. What are you going to add to your shapes? How interesting can you make your work?

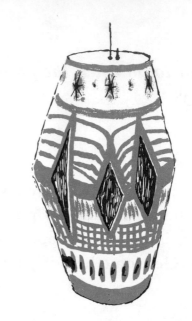

Using a balloon as a mould

The pictures on pages 20 and 21 show some models made on balloons. Most children enjoy using balloons in this way. You can buy balloons of different sizes and shapes. If you are careful, you can use your balloons more than once.

You need a balloon and the same materials as before. (Look on page 14 for the list.)

Blow up your balloon. Tie it very tightly so that no air can escape.

Perhaps you can work together with a friend. You can help one another to tie the balloons if you wish and to hold the balloons while they are being covered.

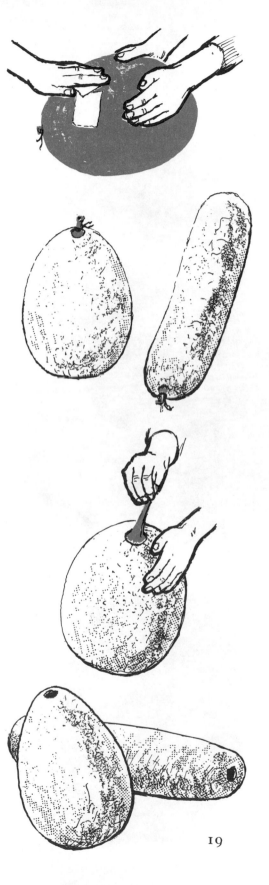

Cover the balloon as you did with the bowl on page 15. Leave a little hole round the neck of the balloon as the picture shows. What is the hole for?

When you have put on all the layers of paper, put your balloon away to dry.

When the paper is dry, hold on to the neck of the balloon and let out the air. Then pull out the balloon. If the balloon does fall inside, you may be able to get it out later.

Have you felt how strong the shape is? What are you going to make with it?

The pictures will give you some ideas, but I hope you will think of some for yourself.

You can cut the shape into pieces if you like. They can be used in many ways. The ship was made from half of a long "sausage" balloon. The other half was used to make something very different. Can you see what was used to make the seats and the mast?

The hedgehog was a balloon with the bottom part of the hedgehog patted flat. Gluing on buttons and bristles from an old brush made him very nice.

At the bottom of the page is a big shape. It was a big balloon covered with paper and then painted. Pieces of the shape were cut out and coloured paper hung inside. Do you like it?

You, too, could decorate a shape made on a balloon. You can use Polyfilla if you want to. Things can be glued and pasted on. You can paint the shape first.

I have seen a lot of exciting things made by children using balloons. The funny fish here was made by Tommy who is only six years old. The owl at the bottom is covered with old nylon stockings.

Have you got your balloon shape ready? Think about what you can do with it. Is it going to be an animal? Are you going to cut it? Is it going to be very gay and hung up in your room? There are hundreds of ways you can work.

Perhaps you will remember this modelling on balloons when you make decorations for a party.

Making your own mould

Have you thought that you could make your own mould? What about making a mould from clay or working on a carving you have done? In this way you will have made everything yourself – the model and the mould.

Modelling on a mould with papier mâché

At the beginning of this book you read about making papier mâché. If you wish, you can use papier mâché to model on a mould.

Press small lumps of mâché on to your mould. Push and press them together to make sure that they stick to one another. When you have covered the mould, put it on one side to dry. You can then paint it or decorate it in other ways.

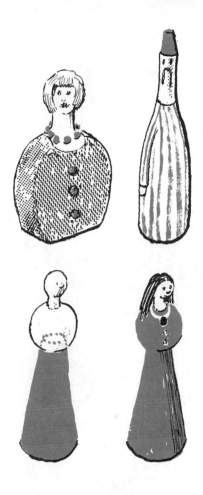

There are times when you can leave the mould inside your model. For instance, the man and woman in the picture were made on old bottles. The bottles were left inside them. You can use squeezy bottles and other odds and ends in this way. Are you going to try?

Opposite is a very interesting figure. She is made from a cardboard cone which came from a factory. Her body was made on a small balloon. Her head was modelled in papier mâché.

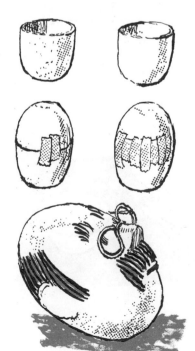

Here are two shapes modelled on egg cups. When they were dry, they were pulled off the cups and glued together. Then as you can see, they were made into a head.

But your shapes need not be heads. Have you got your own ideas? Talk about them. See what you can make.

Working on a mould with string and other things

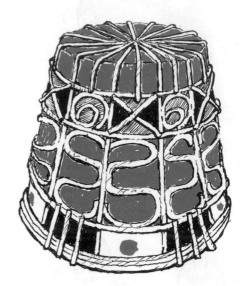

You can work on moulds with many different odds and ends. If you look at the drawing here, you will see a shape made by using string. Why not try using string?

You will need :

String – try string which is not very thin first.
Polyfilla.   A basin, bowl or bucket.   Scissors.
Water.   Toilet paper or tissue paper.   A mould.

Cover the mould with wet toilet paper. Put on plenty of this. Then mix some Polyfilla in the basin or whatever you are using. Do not make it too thick. Do not mix too much at a time. Can you think why?

Decide the length of string you need and cut it. Put it in the basin to cover it with Polyfilla. Then put it on the mould.

24

Make patterns by adding more string covered with Polyfilla. Put on plenty of string. If you leave spaces between which are too big, your shape may collapse.

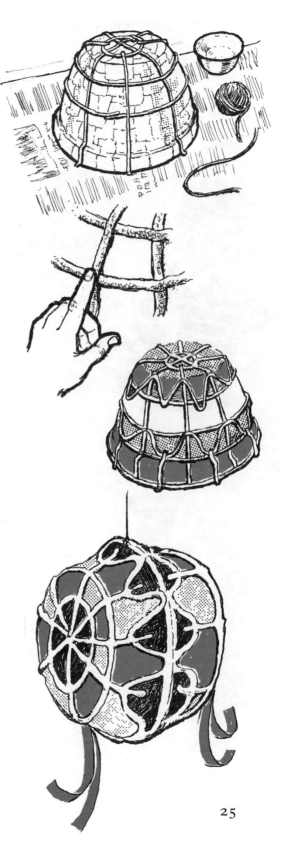

Where your pieces of string cross or touch, press them together. Can you see why? I hope you are thinking about what you are doing. What sort of pattern are you making?

When you have made your pattern as good as you can, let it dry.

When it is dry, lift the shape you have made off the mould. The one in the picture looks very nice with pieces of coloured tissue paper showing behind the string.

Look at the bottom picture! Can you see how this was made? It was used to decorate a room. It looked very good as it twisted round and round on the end of some thin string. Have you noticed that some of the toilet paper has been cut away?

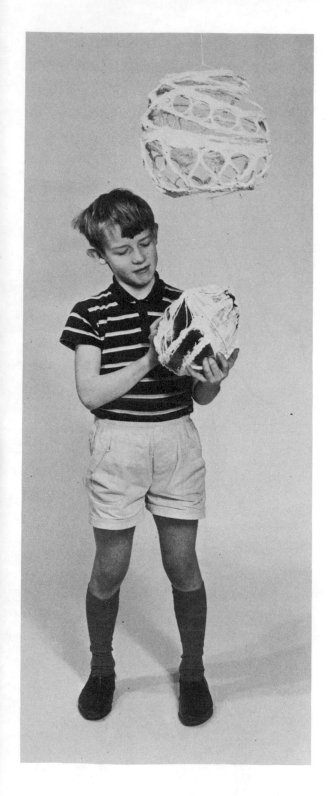

If you haven't guessed yet, I think I should tell you that it was made by making two shapes on a bowl and then fastening them together.

There are more shapes here and at the top of page 27 (opposite).

Try out your own ideas in making string and other shapes. What are you going to use as a mould? What sort of pattern are you going to make?

When you have finished making your shape, can you think of ways of adding things to make it look better? Are you going to work with friends and put your shapes together?

In another book (Book 5 – Making Pictures and Patterns), you can read about making flat patterns with string.

There must be many other odds and ends you can use to work on moulds like this. I am sure you can think of some. Perhaps you have some in your room already. Try them. See what happens. It can be very exciting.

Using starch

Alison is holding a shape which was made from string. (Is it a hat, I wonder?) It was made on a bowl. The string was stiffened with starch instead of Polyfilla.

Do you know what starch is? It is used to stiffen several things. What are these things?

If you have string, a mould and toilet paper, all you need is starch and something to mix it in. You will need some help to mix the starch. Perhaps you are lucky and some nice person has mixed it for you!

Remember to put a layer of toilet paper on the mould. Then pull the string through the starch so that it gets wet all over. Press it on to the mould.

Go on doing this until you have made your pattern. Do you like the one in the picture? Perhaps you can make a better one.

Do you think you could use different sorts of string? What about pieces of wool and tape? Have you other odds and ends you can try?

Now that you have tried using moulds, you may want to use the shapes you have made on them with some of the other things you can make from this book.

I hope you will think of this when you have read about making masks and puppets and the hundreds of other things you can make from odds and ends.

3. *Using Paper Rolls*

Here is a way of building and modelling using magazines or newspapers you have made into rolls. The kangaroo (and its baby) were made from rolls of paper.

You will need:
    Old magazines or newspaper.
    Gummed paper tape.
    You may need other things to decorate what you have made.

Take a sheet of magazine or newspaper and roll it, *as tightly as you can*, into a thin roll. This is how to do it:

Wet your thumb and first finger. Hold a corner of the paper between your thumb and finger. Begin to roll towards the opposite corner. *Press your thumb and finger together hard to keep the roll tight.* When you have rolled a few centimetres, hold the roll while you put it down on your table or desk.

Now roll the paper with both hands. The photographs show you how.

This gets easier when you have made a few rolls. When you get to the corner of the paper, fasten it with a piece of gummed tape (look at the picture). REMEMBER TO KEEP THE ROLLS TIGHT. You will be able to use them better if they are tight. They are much stronger than the loose ones.

Join with a friend and make a lot of these rolls together.

Have you made some? What are you going to make with them? In the pictures 32, 33 and 34, you can see some of the things other children have made.

Here is a good way to start:

Make an oblong by fastening four of the rolls together. Lay one of the rolls across another as the drawing shows. Notice they cross near the end of each roll.

Now fasten the rolls together by using the gummed paper. Wet it and wrap it round and round the place you want to join. Wrap it and fasten it *tightly*. Look at the drawings here. They show you how.

Have you made an oblong? Now fasten another roll across it, from one corner to another, like the one in the picture. Did you know that this is called a diagonal?
Now cut off the ends of the rolls.

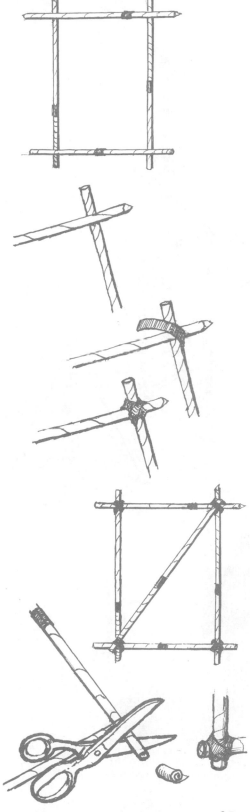

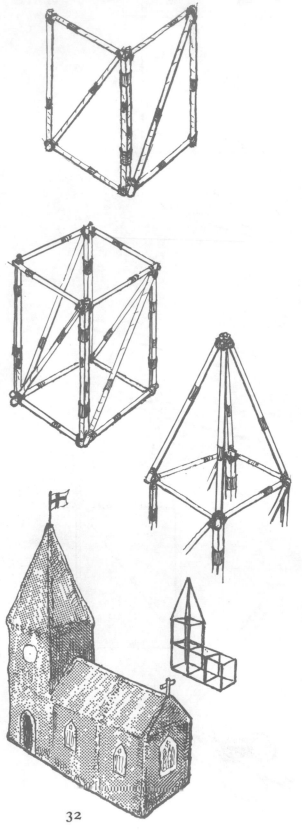

If you make several oblongs like this, you can use them for building. Notice how the oblongs are put together.

The church has a spire. Which part is that? Can you see that the top is made from four rolls? The children who made this covered it with paper and put a cross on it.

Can you see the windows? They were made from coloured tissue paper.

The pictures on pages 33 and 34 will give you some other ideas. But I am sure you will have some of your own.

What are you going to build? Are you going to work together with a friend? You can get on faster if you work together.

More ways of using rolls

There are a lot more models you can make from rolls. The pictures of the animals on this and the next page show some of them. Some of the rolls cannot be seen. They are covered with paper or other things. Some are painted.

One of them has pieces of eggboxes glued on. Another at the top of page 29 has chocolate and toffee papers pasted on. It shines when the light is on it. I wonder what sort of animal it is! An imaginary one no doubt. And what, I wonder, is this one here?

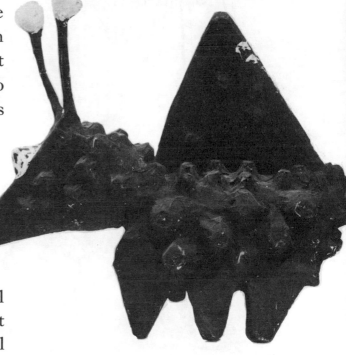

Can you make an imaginary animal or other models? What can you put on the rolls to make your model better? Talk about this.

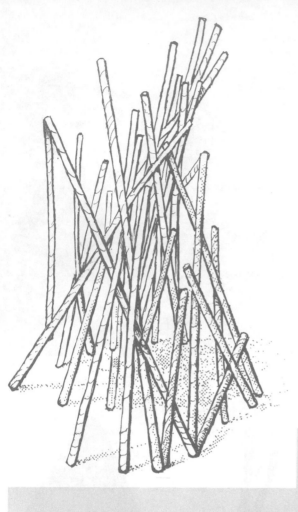

I hope you have noticed the model here. It isn't an animal or bird is it? It is a lot of rolls fastened together. It would be very nice painted. It looks very nice standing or hanging in a room.

I made some of these for a Christmas party. They made the room very jolly. We put up some paper chains as well (like the ones in the book called "Working with Paper", page 74).

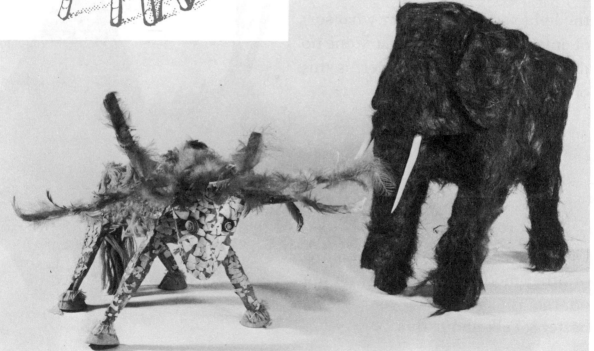

Making a kite with paper rolls

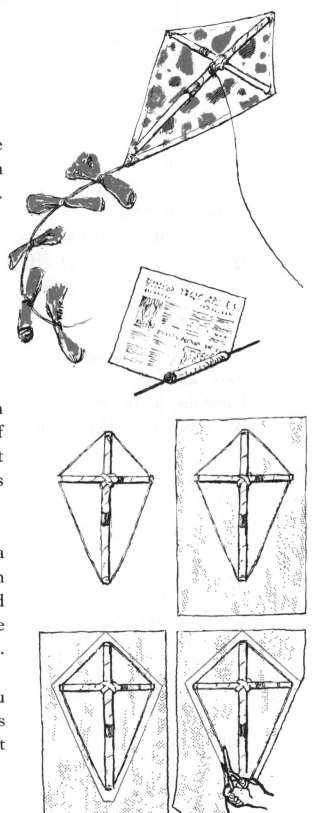

When I was a boy I used to like flying kites. Have you tried flying a kite? You can make one very easily.

You will need :
   Newspaper.   Paste.
   Gummed paper tape.
   A sheet of greaseproof paper.
   String.   Scissors.

Make two paper rolls. Make them very tight to make them strong. If you have some wire you could cut it and roll it inside the paper. This would help to strengthen the roll.

Fasten the rolls in the shape of a cross. Join the ends of the rolls with string as in the drawing. Gummed tape or Sellotape will do. Lay the cross on your greaseproof paper.

Draw a line round the shape you have made, about two centimetres away from the string. Now cut round the line you have drawn.

Turn the edges of the paper over the string and fasten them down. This helps to make the edges stronger.

Fasten on a tail to make your kite fly upright. You can make it from a piece of string. Tie on pieces of paper along the string as the drawing shows. Another sort of tail can be made from lengths of crêpe paper.

If you want, you can make your kite look very nice by printing on it, painting it or pasting on some coloured paper shapes. Perhaps you have other ideas.

You will need a very long string to let your kite fly high. Have you got a ball of string you can use? Some light nylon fishing line is very good, too. Tie one end to your kite (see the drawing). Now you are ready to test it.

It will probably fly best when there is a little wind. If the kite dives down too much, you probably need a longer tail.

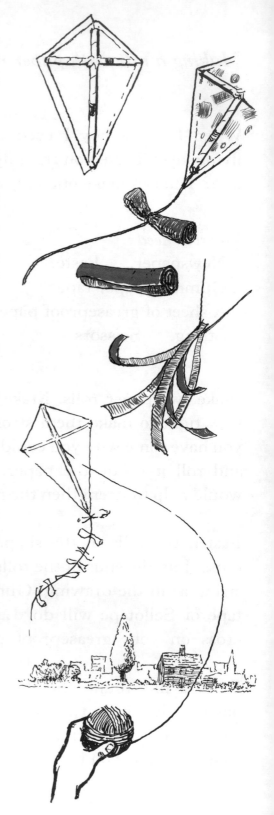

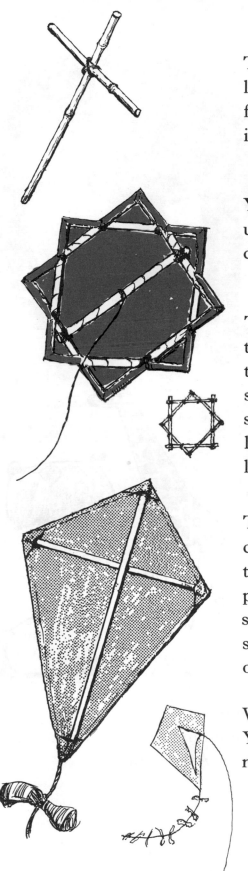

Try tying your string higher or lower on the kite. You should soon find the best place to put it to make it fly well.

You can make a stronger kite by using two thin canes or pieces of dowelling instead of the paper rolls.

There are other shapes you can put together to make a kite. The one in the picture opposite is really two squares fastened together. You can see that it has eight points. It does look strange, but I have seen a kite like this fly very well.

There are other kinds of kite you can make. If you want, you can try to make one from cloth instead of paper. With canes or dowels to stiffen it, it would be a much stronger kite. There is a drawing of one here.

Why not find a book about kites? You may get some good ideas for making them and flying them.

4. *Using Wire and Newspaper*

Newspaper can be pasted on to a wire frame to make good models. The monkey shown here was made in this way. There are some more models on this page which were made in a school. Can you do this, too?

Working together on these models is fun.

You will need :
Newspapers.   Paint.   Paste.
Odds and ends to add to if you want.
Some wire – not too thick.   Something to cut it with. This depends on how thick the wire is.   Ask about this.

Decide what you are going to make. Then make a wire frame. Here is one way of doing this:

Cut pieces of wire. Bend them and fasten them together. The pictures will help you. They show several ways of starting. The wires can be tied together or joined by twisting.

Do you want something with only two legs? How will you make it stand up? Have you thought of a way? The drawings at the bottom show you one way.

You can find a piece of scrap wood for the base. The nails are hammered into the wood, then they are bent over to hold the wire.

Make sure the legs are strong so that they do not bend when you put paper on. How can you make them *really* strong? One way is to fasten several pieces of wire together. The drawings show you how.

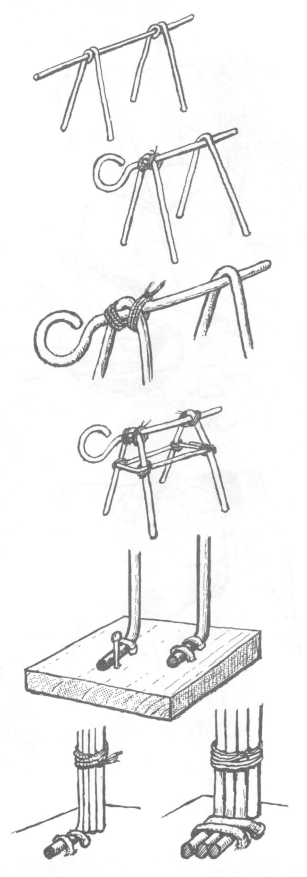

You can save time and paper if you make the frame so that it holds the paper like a skin. This will make the inside of your model hollow.

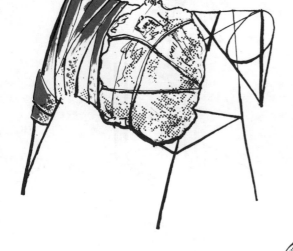

When your frame is ready, paste on small pieces or strips of paper. Overlap them and cover all the frame. Where you need to build up the model, paste on more paper. The drawings will help you.

If you need to make part of your model bigger very quickly, you can add folded paper. Roll pieces of paper like a parcel. Fasten them to the frame with gummed paper or string. Then you can paste paper on top.

Keep looking at your work and asking yourself where you need to add more paper to make it better.

Look at the poor elephant here! He has lumps and hollows on his body. He would be better if more paper were put on to make him smoother.

When you have made your model, you can cover it with coloured paper or paint it. Perhaps you will want to fasten on other odds and ends to improve it.

What are you going to do to make your model better? Think about it. See what you have or can find to use.

The zoo animals on this page were made in this way.

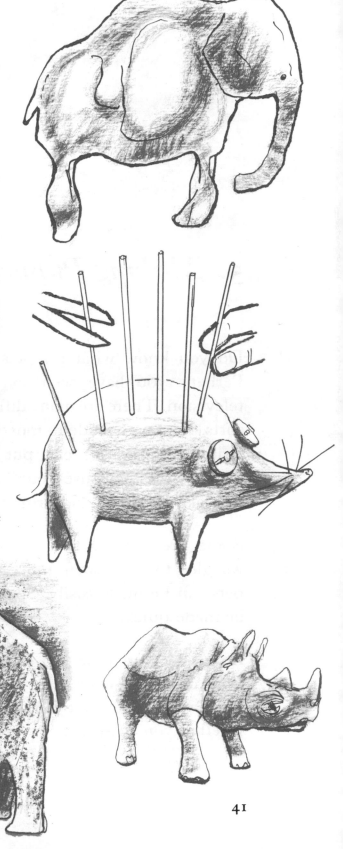

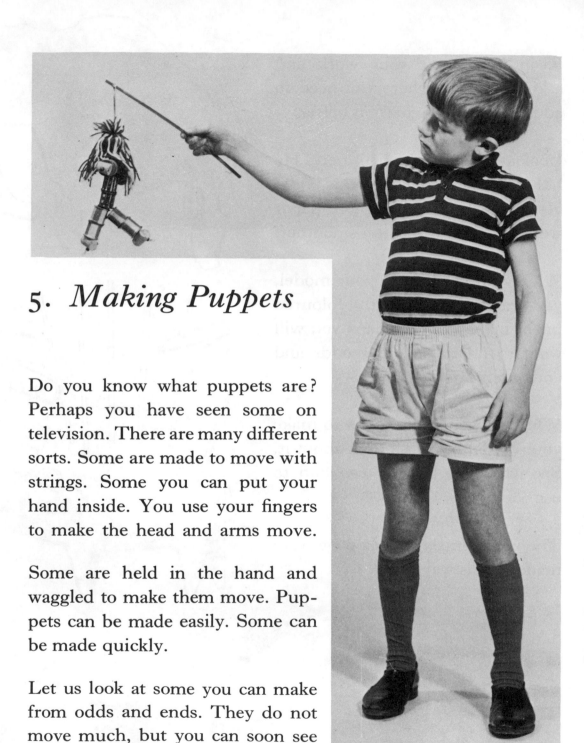

5. Making Puppets

Do you know what puppets are? Perhaps you have seen some on television. There are many different sorts. Some are made to move with strings. Some you can put your hand inside. You use your fingers to make the head and arms move.

Some are held in the hand and waggled to make them move. Puppets can be made easily. Some can be made quickly.

Let us look at some you can make from odds and ends. They do not move much, but you can soon see whether you like them.

Paper bag puppets

Have you a paper bag? You need one big enough to put your hand into. If you look at the photograph, you can see that the bag has had its middle tied with string.

Pieces of paper have been stuck on to make eyes, nose and mouth. Some parts have been painted. Perhaps a bag could be printed on too? What do you think? Can you make a paper bag puppet?

Newspaper puppet

This is another easy one to make. One or two small sheets of newspaper or magazine are tied over a squeezed-up lump of paper. How would you make this look like a head?

A sock puppet

Paper bags and newspapers soon tear. Here is another easy way to make a stronger puppet. It moves its head when you put your hand inside and move it up, down and sideways.

You will need :
    An old sock.
    An ice cream or other container.
    Odds and ends to make a face (buttons, wool or whatever you want).

Push the container into the toe of the sock. If you want, you can turn up the very end of the toe and glue it or stitch it. It could help to make a nose or a mouth. The pictures show how it is made.

This one has buttons for eyes, but you may want to use other odds and ends. Are you going to put ears on? The puppet in the picture *is* rather nice, isn't he? Is he a dog or a horse, I wonder?

A mouth puppet

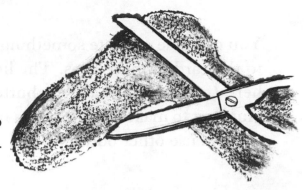

Another way of using a sock is to cut off the toe part and put something in it to make a big mouth.

You will need :

  An old sock or piece of cloth.
  Cardboard.
  Paint and paper.
  Paste or glue.

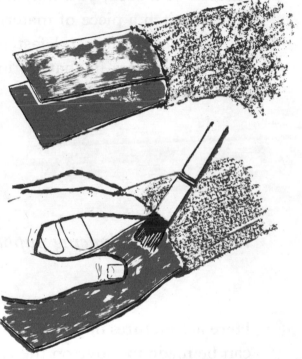

Have you cut the sock? Now cut the cardboard so that the pieces fit tightly into the sock as in the drawing. Push the card in until you can put your hand into the other end of the sock and hold the ends of the cardboard. The pictures show how.

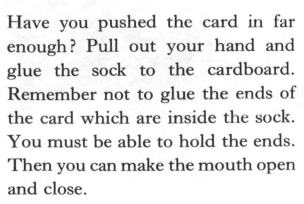

Have you pushed the card in far enough? Pull out your hand and glue the sock to the cardboard. Remember not to glue the ends of the card which are inside the sock. You must be able to hold the ends. Then you can make the mouth open and close.

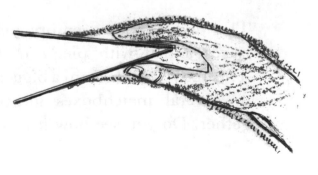

You can glue or paste something on to the card to make eyes. The head here (what is it?) has two buttons glued on to make eyes. But you may want to use other odds and ends.

Instead of a sock, you may like to glue or stitch a piece of material in the form of a tube and fasten the cardboard pieces in that, as in the photograph.

Waggling and dancing puppets

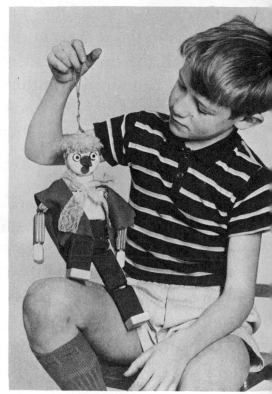

Here are pictures of puppets which can be made to move on the end of a stick or on string.

The first one uses empty matchboxes joined with pieces of tape. The body is made from a bigger box or several matchboxes glued together. Do you see how it is done?

It was covered by pasting on pieces of cloth, but other things could be used. He could be painted. Hold the stick and make him waggle!

The dancing girl was made from cream and ice cream cartons. The arms and legs are hair curlers.

The lively lad with long hair was a washing-up mop. The picture shows how the mop was fastened to make a head. The body, legs and arms are pieces of cardboard fastened together with tape. The cardboard was covered with pieces cut from an old pair of pyjamas.

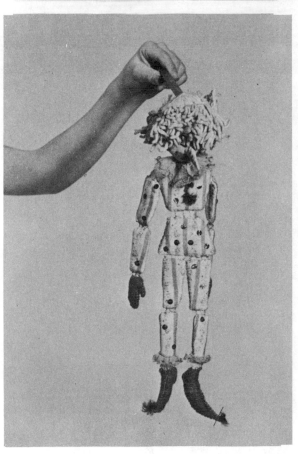

Of course, you can use other things. What have you got? What ideas have you thought of?

Be a snake charmer

This snake looks alive when the stick is held so that the tail touches the ground. Move the string about and the snake dances.

Old cotton reels are threaded and tied with string. There is a knot between each reel. The body is covered with cloth. You can glue the edges together. The eyes are beads. A girl made this one and stitched the side together instead of gluing it.

Glove puppets

There are different ways of making a body but the shape here will do. Make it so that it fits easily over your hand. You can stitch or glue the edges together.

Roll a piece of thin card and glue it. A piece of old postcard or birthday card would be good. Make it so that it slides on to your finger.

The head of the puppet is put on the end of the roll. The other end is fastened into the body as in the drawing.

You can make the head in different ways. On page 11 you can read how to make one from papier mâché. But you can find many other useful things for heads: a table tennis ball, a small ball of wool, cardboard tube (part of a toilet roll), and so on. What can you find to use?

I wonder what puppets you will make? I think you could make some very good ones.

49

Rod puppets

There are two rod puppets in the picture here. Perhaps you can guess how they are used.

Rod puppets have been made for hundreds of years. They are still used in some parts of the world. Often they are used to make shadows on a screen. What do you think such a puppet is called? There is one here on this page. It came from Java. Which one is it? Why do you think it looks as though it is Javanese?

Rod puppets which move arms and legs can be difficult to make. Ask your teacher about them. Can you find a book about them? Perhaps you can find out which countries still have lots of puppet plays.

There are many other ways of making puppets from odds and ends. The photograph shows some of the puppets I have got. But only some. You see, I have more than fifty of them!

In the photograph, the soldier was made from a plastic bottle with a handle. The head came from a round box. It was cut to shape and then a peg was fastened in it. The peg goes into the neck of the bottle. Perhaps you can see or guess how the others were made.

If you try, you can make a lot of different puppets. What about putting on a show? You can make puppets to act the parts in a play or story.

You may know a suitable story, or you may wish to write your own play. Discuss this. You can have a lot of fun.

A theatre for puppets

To have your own puppet theatre is a good idea. There are many you can make. They can be different sizes. You could use chairs, a broom handle and some material for curtains. The one in the drawing at the top of this page is very different. It was made from a large box. I think it was a shirt box.

You could make this yourself, but it is fun to make one with friends. Decide who is going to make the different things you will need. What sort of theatre will it be? What sort of scene will it be? Will it be in a town or in the country?

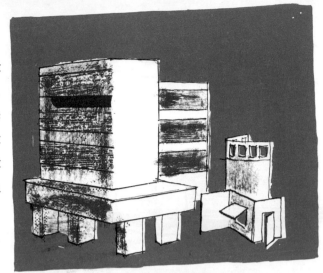

Then you will need to talk about the many things you are going to put in the scene. Will there be a house, a castle, some trees, or what?

Could you paint the things you want on paper and cut them out? What about sticking your cut-outs into small pieces of wood or small lumps of plasticine? Are you going to put some little models in? There are so many things you could do to make a really good theatre.

53

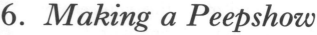

6. *Making a Peepshow*

What have you been reading about or hearing about in the last few days? Perhaps you have been reading about Eskimoes or about the desert or life under the sea. As well as making paintings or drawings, you could make a peepshow.

You will need :

A shoe box and lid.

Scissors or a knife.

Bits of tissue paper or cellophane.

Odds and ends – bits of twigs, used matches, bits of sponge – anything to help you build the scene in a box.

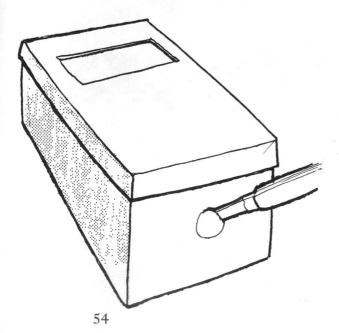

First cut a hole with your scissors or knife in the middle of one end of the box, as the drawing shows. Then cut a round or oblong hole in the lid at one end.

With the lid off, build a scene in the bottom of the box. Keep looking through the hole in the end of the box to see what it looks like. Notice how different things look when seen through a hole.

Put the lid on to see whether the hole is letting in enough light. The hole in the lid needs to be at the end opposite your peephole.

What sort of a scene are you making? Is it a rough sea of crumpled paper and a ship with matches for masts? Perhaps it is a matchbox house with a piece of mirror for a lake and a bit of old sponge on a twig to make a tree. Try out different things.

You will have a lot of ideas of how to make your scene look real and exciting when you peep through the hole. Remember to put on the lid each time you peep.

Try putting pieces of tissue paper or cellophane over the hole in the lid. Cellophane is best if you have it.

What happens to the light? How do different colours change the scene? How can the colour make your scene look cold or warm or stormy?

What else can you put into your box? You could have things hanging down from the lid – birds or aeroplanes on threads of cotton, for example.

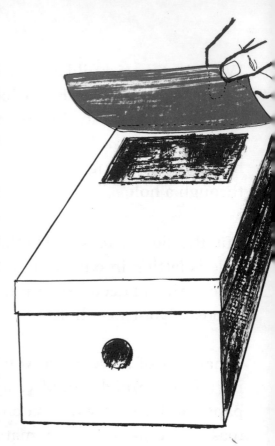

Is someone else making a peepshow? What does it look like? Let them look at yours. What kind of strange world can you see?

Jim has done something different with his peepshow. He has cut a hole in the side and can shine a torch through it just like a spotlight in a theatre. Some parts get a lot of light and others are in shadow. It looks very dramatic in his box.

What would happen if he shone his light from a hole on the other side? Are you going to try Jim's idea or other things?

7. *Making Masks*

In other books ("Working with Paper" and "Modelling, Building and Carving") you can read about making masks with clay or card or paper. Here are two more ways of making masks, using odds and ends. You might need masks quickly for a play or a party.

You will need :

> An old paper bag big enough to go over your head.
> Paint.
> Scraps of tissue paper or other odds and ends.

DO NOT USE A POLYTHENE BAG. I am sure you have been told how dangerous that would be.

Put the paper bag over your head. Gently feel where your eyes come and mark the places with a piece of sticky paper on the outside of the bag.

Take the bag off your head. With the bag on a table or desk and NOT on your head, make holes for your eyes where you have marked.

Now you can paint a face on the bag. Keep the paint thick so that it doesn't run down the paper. Is the face gay or sad? Is the person you are painting fat or thin, mean or generous? How can you show these things on your mask?

Perhaps some one will pull faces for you – sad ones, surprised ones and so on. See what sort of lines they make on their faces. What sort of shapes appear? Perhaps you have a mirror and can pull faces yourself!

If you have some paste and tissue paper, you could paste the bag and then put on the tissue paper. Try pushing it and sliding it about on the bag. It can make lines and ridges and shapes you want for your face. Why not try fastening on other odds and ends?

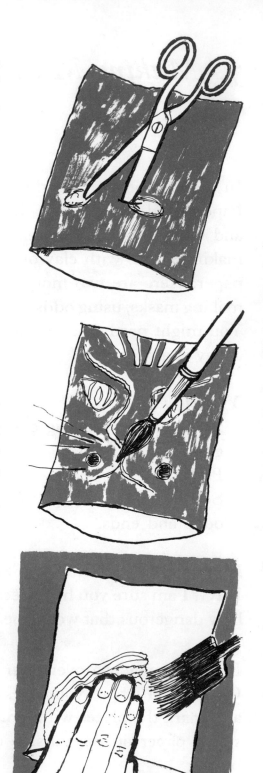

58

My children made some lovely masks for a play using big cardboard tubes. The photograph shows two of them.

Rolls of lino and other floor covering often come to the shops on tubes like these. Some are about twenty centimetres in diameter and two metres long. Shopkeepers throw these tubes away. We were given some and sawed them up into pieces. They fitted over the heads of the actors like helmets. (Perhaps you would like to make a helmet!)

Then odds and ends were fastened on to make these strange creatures. Can you see what the teeth are made from?

Try out your ideas for making masks. What sort of people or creatures are you going to make? What have you got which you can use?

8. *Using String, Pipe Cleaners and Drinking Straws*

The things in the pictures here were made with string.

You will need :

String of different thicknesses. (If you can find string of different colours as well, then all the better.)

Scissors.

Raffia and cotton can be useful if you have them and some pieces of rope – clothes line perhaps.

You can try several ways of modelling with string. Here is one way. Take a piece of string, not too thin, about thirty centimetres long. Put it down on your table or desk in this sort of shape, with the loop at the bottom. This forms the body and arms.

Then take another piece, like the first, and bend it like the other shape – the one with the loop at the top. Bind it with thin string or nylon as the drawing shows. This will make the head and legs.

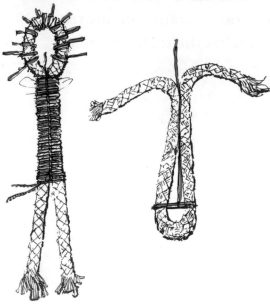

Bind them tightly together round the middle with thin string or raffia or cotton or nylon which is very tough.

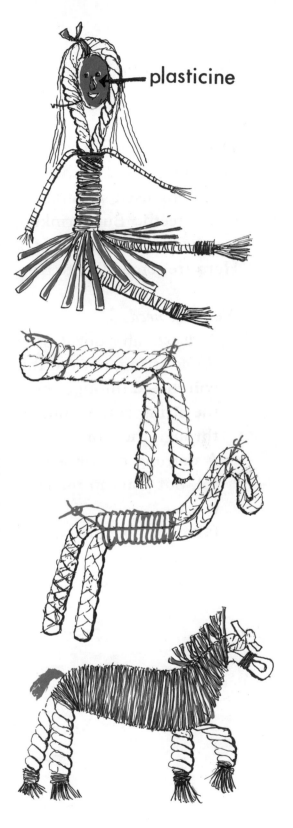

plasticine

Now you will have the beginning of a little string figure or puppet. In the pictures, little pieces of odds and ends have been fastened on. One has had little blobs of paint added.

The horse was made in the same way. A thick piece of string or rope made the head, legs, neck and body. Thinner pieces fastened it all together. The drawings will help you to see how it was done. The body was wrapped round and round with raffia. Notice the mane. How do you think that was made?

What sort of string have you got? The size and thickness may make you decide to make bigger or smaller things. Big things might be difficult with thin string. Try out different things and ways of making them. You will do better if you try more than one thing.

Drinking straws

Drinking straws can be used to decorate things. On page 7 you can see them used in small pieces to make teeth. But drinking straws can be the main part of a model. Here are some ideas to try.

You will need :
>   At least half a dozen straws.
>   Some string, not too thin, which will thread through the straws. If the string is too thin, it may cut through the straws.
>   A darning needle would be useful, but you can manage without it.
>   Glue – rubber glue would be best.
>   Tissue paper or cellophane.
>   Scissors.   Sellotape.

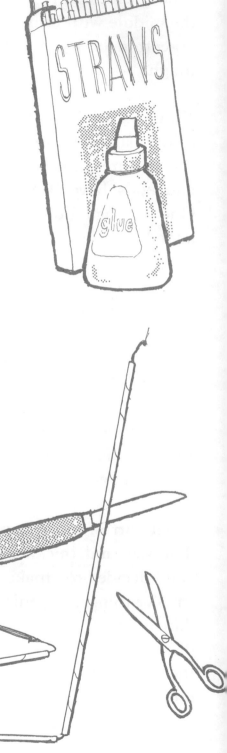

The little star was a Christmas decoration and was made by gluing down some straws on the back side of coloured tissue paper and then cutting round the straws.

The hanging decoration at the bottom was made by threading string through three straws at a time to make a triangle or four straws to make a diamond. Push the straws along the string and then fasten the ends of the string together. The diamonds and the triangles were fastened together with paper clips.

There are many more ways you can use drinking straws. One way of using squashed straws is to plait them (look at the drawing on the right). What other ways can you find?

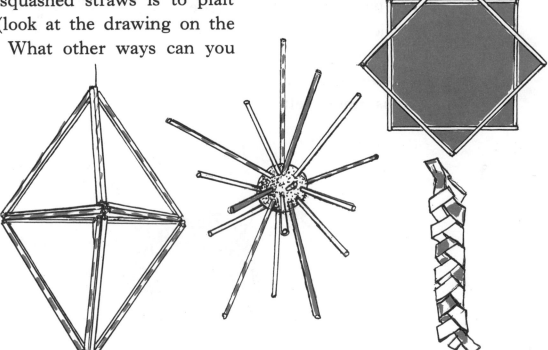

Pipe cleaners

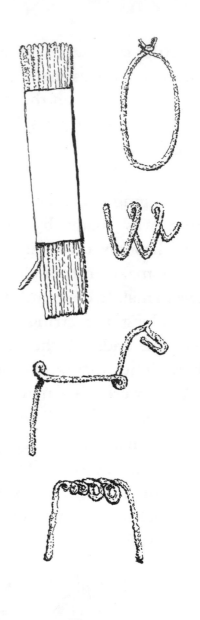

You can make things with pipe cleaners, too. The little horse and rider opposite were made from them. Pipe cleaners are cheap and are pieces of soft wire about fifteen centimetres long, covered in fluffy woolly material. The wire bends easily. I use them for cleaning the stem of my pipe.

The horse was made from three cleaners. The first was bent into the shape of the drawing here.

The second was twisted round the first piece to form a front leg, the body and a back leg. Notice that the cleaner is laid across the first to allow about two centimetres for the leg. Then it is twisted round and round until there is enough left for another leg.

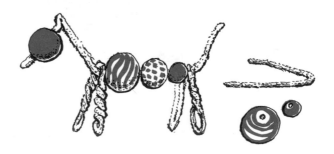

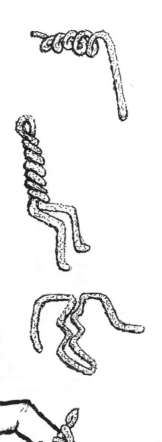

The third cleaner is used in the same way. It was twisted round the other two to make the other front leg, more of the body and the second back leg.

The rider was made from two pieces. They were shaped like these in the drawings. They were then twisted together to make the rider. It was quite easy to sit him on the horse.

Perhaps you would like to try and make other things from pipe cleaners. You can think of some, I'm sure. Here are some I have made.

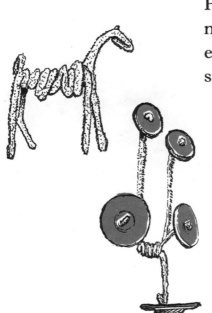

9. *Making Models and Things from Scrap*

A lot of odds and ends are really *scrap*. Scrap is the name given to things we throw away because we have no further use for them. But very often scrap *can* be used. I have seen children make many lovely models from scrap.

Such things as squeezy bottles, date boxes, egg cartons, milk and other bottle tops, cotton reels and many others can often be used. So keep a box full of things which you might be able to use in your work.

On this and the next pages, you will find some very interesting models which are all made from scrap or odds and ends. When you have seen how they are made, I hope you will look at your collection of scrap and make some of your own models.

First of all, here is a fine helicopter. It was made from a Smartie tube, a strawberry punnet, some cellophane from a box of chocolates and two toilet roll cores.

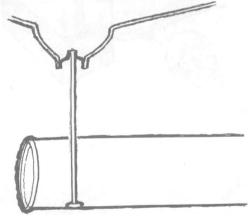

The rotor blades were made from a squeezy bottle.

The drawing shows how the bottle cap was glued onto the blades and put on the end of a knitting needle.

This transporter is painted red and black and looks very good. It is mainly two pieces of wood from a date box. The cab and bonnet are a small tin like a mustard tin. Can you see what the wheels are? The drawing shows how they are fastened on. The windscreen and the glass of the cab are pieces of white paper stuck on to the tin.

On page 68, Jim has an engine made from a tin can, boot polish tins, cotton reels and cardboard.

The car at the top of this page is a cardboard box. The wheels are slices off a sponge paint-roller.

The tortoise is an empty silver paper pie dish and a lot of metal caps from bottles. Some newspaper was glued to the bottom of the pie dish, as in the drawing, after a hole had been cut in the side for the head.

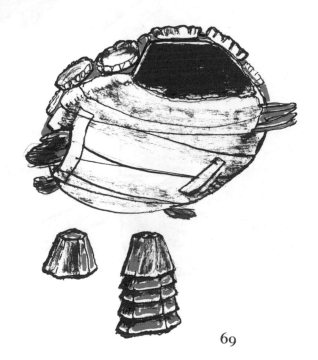

The metal caps were glued on. The head is made from egg cartons cut up. When the glue was dry, the caps were painted.

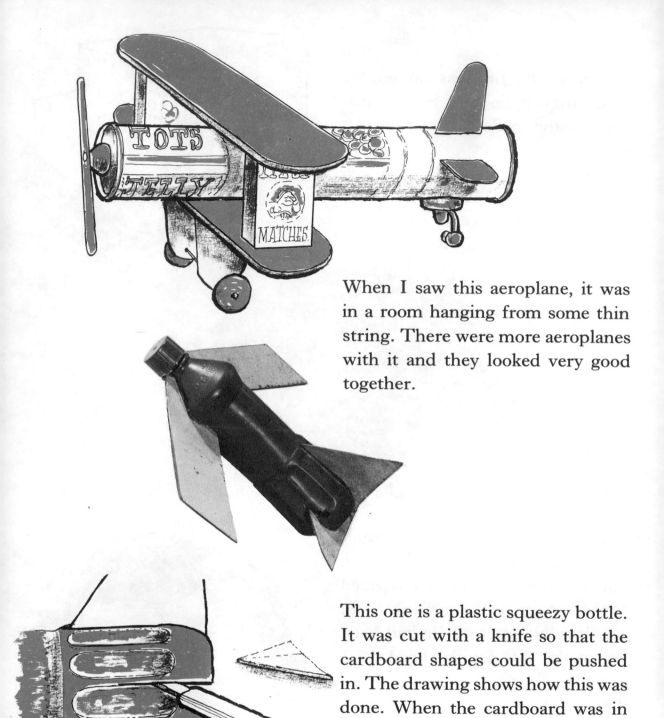

When I saw this aeroplane, it was in a room hanging from some thin string. There were more aeroplanes with it and they looked very good together.

This one is a plastic squeezy bottle. It was cut with a knife so that the cardboard shapes could be pushed in. The drawing shows how this was done. When the cardboard was in place, some glue was dabbed on to make sure that the wings and tail did not drop out.

Here is a lion in a cage. Have you ever seen one? The picture shows the lion drawn bigger and outside the cage. He *is* rather a funny lion isn't he? He is really a cotton reel with wire legs wrapped in wool and some wool for his tail and mane. The eyes are painted on.

The cage is a piece of scrap wood with wheels made from wooden buttons. They are screwed or nailed on. Holes were made in the wheels first. A screw was used to fasten them on. The drawing shows you how.

To make a really good job, the drawings show you how to fasten on two small pieces of wood. The wheels can be screwed into these pieces.

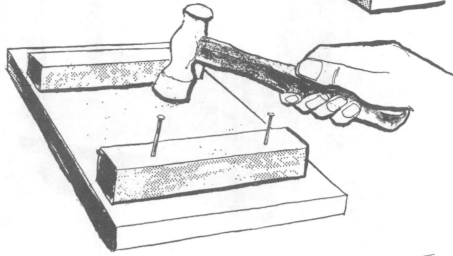

The bars of the cage are pieces of wire. They can be coloured to make the cage look very gay. Four narrow strips of card make the top edge of the bars. Yes, the wires are glued to them.

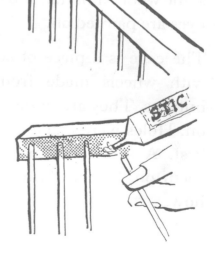

Do you like this model? It looks very nice and I would rather see this sort of lion in a cage than a real live one.

Egg boxes are very useful for all kinds of modelling and building. If you can collect some, they are worth keeping somewhere ready for when you need them.

Here is a crocodile made from egg boxes. They are fastened together with glue and sellotape. If you look at the pictures you can see how it is done. The tail is made thinner towards the end by squeezing the cartons. The eyes are big buttons and the legs are foam sponge glued on.

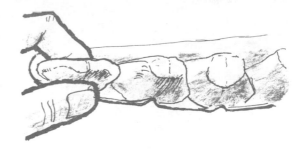

Mr. Crocodile is very handsome, he is painted green. On another crocodile the jaws opened like this.

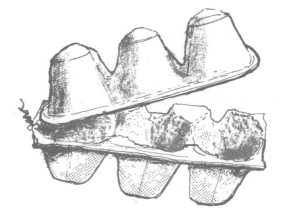

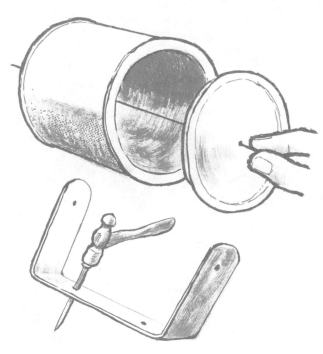

Two tin cans and two cardboard boxes made most of this road roller. You can see that one of the boxes is cut to make the cab. The boxes are glued together. Both the tin cans had holes made in their bottoms and in their lids.

If you make the holes, but leave the lids off, you can put some wire through quite easily to make axles. Push the wire through the hole in the bottom of the can as the drawing shows. Push it so that it sticks out of the top of the can.

Now put the lid on to the wire and press it into the can opening just as though you were closing the can.

The rollers in this model are held on with strips of tin but cardboard can be used, too.

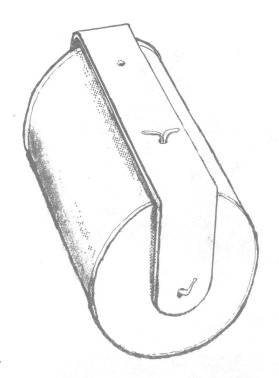

A little box is glued at the front of the roller as you can see. To make it look really good, the roller is painted in gay colours.

Now you have read about these scrap models, are you going to try making your own models? I am sure that when you have collected your scrap you will have many different ideas. Try them and see whether you, too, can make some models as good as, or better than these.

A lot of scrap and odds and ends can be used to make very good decorations. On this page are two of the decorations I made for Christmas. They turned and swung in the air as they hung from the lights in the room.

This first one was made from five fruit trays obtained from a green-grocer. They were fastened together at the ends as you can see. The middle was filled with tissue paper. Other things could be used, perhaps a balloon.

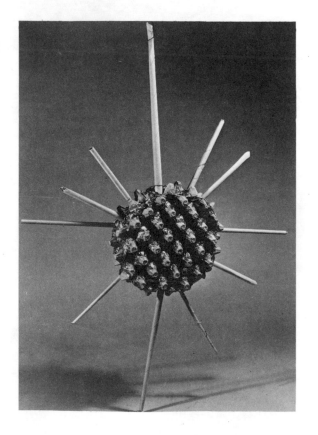

The next one has paper rolls. These were covered with silver paper to glisten in the light. The middle was made from pieces of egg tray and later the ends of the paper rolls were joined by tinsel glued on. Lovely!

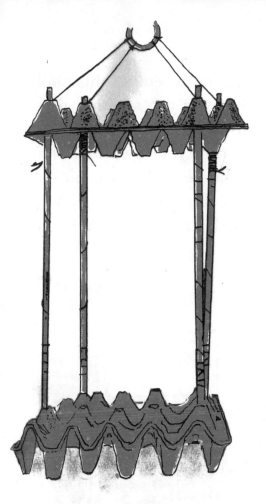

The third one was made from paper rolls which were pushed through two fruit or egg trays. (Did you know that many of these trays are made from papier mâché?) Gummed paper tape was fastened round the rolls and on to the trays so that the trays did not slide off. Strips of coloured paper were pasted on to make the thing look gay.

Do these make you think about *your* decorations? What have you to put together to make a room look gay? Go ahead and make decorations from your odds and ends.

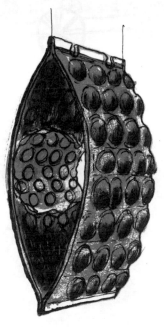

So we come to the end of this book. I hope that you can see that there are a lot of uses for odds and ends and scrap. Try your own ideas and see what happens. Do not be discouraged if things go wrong. A lot of the models I made went wrong at first.

Go back in the book to read again about using odds and ends.

You can get a lot of enjoyment trying things out and you will get better as you go on.

Index